Know About
Mental Illness

Know About Mental Illness

Margaret O. Hyde
and
Elizabeth H. Forsyth, M.D.

Walker and Company
New York

First published in the United States of America in 1996 by Walker Publishing Company, Inc.

Published simultaneously in Canada by Thomas Allen & Son Canada, Limited, Markham, Ontario

Library of Congress Cataloging-in-Publication Data
Hyde, Margaret O. (Margaret Oldroyd)
    Know about mental illness / Margaret O. Hyde and Elizabeth H. Forsyth.
        p.   cm.
    Includes bibliographical references and index.
    Summary: Discusses many aspects of mental illness, including types, causes, cures, and misconceptions.
    ISBN 0-8027-8428-3 (hardcover). —ISBN 0-8027-8429-1 (reinforced)
    1. Mental illness—Juvenile literature.   [1. Mental illness.]
I. Forsyth, Elizabeth Held.   II. Title.
RC460.2.H93   1996
616.89—dc20   95-50114
                                                                    CIP
                                                                    AC

Printed in the United States of America

10   9   8   7   6   5   4   3   2   1

Contents

Acknowledgments

Some of the drawings in this book have been made by students at the August Aichhorn Center for Adolescent and Residential Care, Inc., in New York City. Residents of the school have small classes in which they study math, social studies, English, career education, and art. Painting, sculpting, drawing, and any type of creativity can be part of the therapy for young people with emotional problems. Students in the art classes engage in projects that reflect on self-awareness, achievement, and personal growth. When the students go to class, they lose themselves in their work. Sometimes the stories that children tell about their drawings give therapists clues about what troubles them.

As shown in the illustrations in this book, some of these students show special talent.

The authors wish to thank Mat Holmes, child care worker/assistant art teacher at the August Aichhorn Center, for providing drawings and Mary Hill for her helpful suggestions.

1.

Mental Illness Here, There, and Everywhere

"**I**s she crazy?" "He has a screw loose." "That's insane." You probably hear expressions like this all the time. They seldom refer to anyone who is mentally ill. You may have met and heard about many people who really suffer from various kinds of mental illness, even though you may not know it. Some well-known figures such as Ludwig van Beethoven, Winston Churchill, Abraham Lincoln, Michelangelo, and Isaac Newton suffered from severe mental illness. You may have some emotional problems yourself without realizing that they are serious enough to be considered a mental illness.

More than three million children and adolescents who have difficulty making friends, learning, or controlling their emotions have a treatable chemical imbalance in their brains. One-third of all Americans will suffer a serious mental problem at some time in their lives, but many of them will feel too ashamed about it to go for help.

According to experts, about one in four patients who seek medical help for physical problems actually have an undetected mental disorder. Many of these people become ill when they are teens, but they do not feel comfortable talking to someone about it. They need to know that it is okay to talk to a counselor or a therapist about difficult feelings. Their families need to know how to help them and how to deal with the problems they bring to the lives of each relative.

Today, many adults talk freely about seeing specialists who treat those who are troubled. Public service announcements on television send the message that people with mental illnesses can get help, and that many can return to school, work again, and live well. But there are still large numbers of people who think only of the most severely ill in connection with mental illness.

Mental illness can affect the ability to think, to feel, and to relate to other people and one's surroundings. Some serious kinds of mental illness cause people to be so confused at times that they live in an unreal world. Doctors say they are *psychotic.* Joe is a schizophrenic child who often gets angry for no reason that anyone else can understand. Joe believes there is a little man in his stomach who makes him do bad things, such as telling him to drown the cat. (For a discussion of *schizophrenia,* see chapters 5 and 6.)

While most mental disorders do not cause psychotic symptoms, they all cause pain and distress.

Sometimes there is no clear dividing line between normal and abnormal, but some types of mental illness are so severe that they are easy to recognize. This is true for children like Joe and in the case of Polly, who suffers from *depression* (discussed at length in chapter 7). She stays in bed all day because she says she is too tired to do anything else. She believes she is stupid and ugly; she feels worthless and sometimes thinks about killing herself. Polly suffers from severe depression.

For many years, people with mental illness were blamed for their disorders and considered "tainted" because their diseases were misunderstood. Some of those feelings still remain. But people need to know that many of the mysteries of mental illnesses have been unraveled by researchers. Changes in the balance of chemicals or differences in brain structure have been found to cause some kinds of mental illness. Yet when chemical imbalance or abnormal development causes disease in other parts of the body, those diseases are more easily accepted.

Much of the stigma of mental illness is based on fear and lack of knowledge. Alexa and Sue were in sixth grade when they met a boy named Josh who had been mentally ill. Some kids in their class said that Josh was crazy, but Alexa liked him. She wondered if she should be afraid of Josh, but he seemed caring and he was very bright. Sometimes he made her laugh. Sue told Alexa to be careful about getting close to Josh because he had been in the "nuthouse." Actually, Josh had suffered from severe depression three years earlier when his parents were getting a divorce, and he had spent a month in a hospital for people who are emotionally ill. For the next year, he talked with a psychiatrist every two weeks.

Josh and his brothers lived with their mother during the week and with their father on weekends. The trauma of the divorce was behind him, and Josh was quite healthy mentally as well as physically. Now he had many friends who accepted his earlier problems, even though people like Sue avoided him. Josh was a kind person who was always ready to help others, but Sue and kids like her knew so little about mental illness that it frightened them and kept them from getting to know the real Josh.

Sue thinks that everyone who has ever been in a hospital for any kind of emotional problem is probably going to do something weird, or even violent. She tells a story about a man who walked into a park where a girl was sitting on a bench reading a book. The man, who had just been released from the local mental hospital, had stopped taking his medicine and was hearing voices. The voices told him to hit the girl, so he hit her on the head with a piece of pipe—and killed her. This kind of thing is very tragic, but it is also rare. It is the kind of story that people never forget, and helps spread the idea that mentally ill people are dangerous. Many people think that you can never tell what "crazy" people will do. They put all the mentally ill in one group, no matter whether their problems are severe or minor. They don't realize that most mentally ill people are not violent, but subdued and withdrawn. Many violent people are not mentally ill.

Through the years, the mentally ill have been treated as if they were responsible for seeing things in a different way from most of the world. Their problems may be the result of differences in the way their brains work or wrong ideas that they learned while growing up, or a combination of these factors. Because they are different, and in some cases unpleasant, people often feel embarrassed when a member of their family is mentally ill.

Twelve-year-old Sara wishes her older brother, Mike, suffered from a disease like tuberculosis instead of *obsessive-compulsive disorder* (see discussion in chapter 4). He washes his hands about twenty times a day. He wears a mask when there is a stranger in the house because he is afraid of new germs, and he fears that he is being exposed to "all kinds of germs" at school. Sara's friends tease her about whether or not they should wear a mask when they visit her. If Mike had some "real disease" that was caused by some kind of bacteria or virus, everyone would understand him better. But Mike's disease seems silly, and the kids call him "crazy." Some experts believe patients with conditions like his have disturbances in brain chemistry. Sara's friends could accept Mike's actions better if they knew this was the case, or even if they tried to understand what Mike feels.

Many people are aware that people with mental disorders are troubled, perplexed human beings who deserve as much sensitivity and love as people who suffer from cancer, heart disease, multiple sclerosis, or a broken back. The brain is an organ that can suffer from disease much as the back and heart can.

Unfortunately, mental illness has been so mysterious throughout history that shame, guilt, and punishment have been connected with it. This is often still true today. One grandmother of a girl who is suffering from depression called a friend to find out where she could learn more about the girl's condition. But she made her friend promise not to tell anyone that this granddaughter had problems. She had some good reasons for this, since many people would think less of the girl for being depressed. Only 20 percent of the seriously depressed seek help. This is especially tragic since doctors can relieve their suffering in most cases.

Karen A. Kangas, director of community education for the Connecticut Department of Mental Health, suggests that if everyone who is mentally ill told someone about it at noon, the stigma about mental illness would be over by 12:30 P.M. People would know that mental illness is everywhere. No one is immune from mental suffering, and few families are without a member who suffers from one or more of the numerous mental disorders that afflict human beings.

One of the most famous people who suffered serious mental illness was Vincent van Gogh. He wrote the following in a letter to his brother, Theo: "As for me, you must know I shouldn't precisely have chosen madness if there had been any choice. What consoles me is that I am beginning to consider madness as an illness like any other, and that I accept it as such." Van Gogh painted a beautiful arrangement of irises in the asylum garden at St. Remy in 1889. Today, a number of groups use this flower as an emblem in their crusades against mental illness.

Friends and family members of the mentally ill formed an organization in 1979 to help reduce the stigma of mental illness. Known as the National Alliance for the Mentally Ill (NAMI), it is dedicated to improving the lives of those with mental illness. Some members of NAMI volunteer on its Anti-Stigma Network, a group which responds quickly to items in the press and other media that stigmatize the mentally ill. For example, the Anti-Stigma Network persuaded the creators of Superman to cancel their plans to let an escapee from a mental institution kill off the man of steel. Because of their work, comic books have changed plotlines of their stories, roles of players in soap operas have been rewritten, and comedians who use "crazy" people as the brunt of their jokes have rewritten their monologues.

Many people in society do not realize the extent to which stigma can harm the treatment and recovery of the mentally ill. While some people enjoy making fun of them, others use accurate information and understanding to spread the truth. Newspapers, magazines, and television and radio programs offer the best hope of reducing the stigma. Rather than showing only the homeless person huddled in the alley who talks to himself and the woman with multiple personalities, they can show people who have recovered from mental illness and promote understanding and acceptance of persons with histories of mental illness.

Even though most people have wrong ideas about it, mental illness has been called the number one health problem in the United States today. At least 12 percent of all American children suffer from mental disorders. Helping these children early can make a huge difference in their lives and in those of their families.

During the last few decades, scientific research has changed much of the understanding of mental illness. Very effective drugs have been developed for treating people with mental illness, enabling them to lead normal lives. Knowing more about mental illness can help everyone to be more understanding.

2.

From the Devil to a Pill

If you were mentally ill in ancient times, your strange behavior would probably have been blamed on evil spirits. You might have been accused of being possessed by the devil as punishment for your sins. Or you might have been accused of being an instrument of the devil, who used you to cause floods and other terrible things. This was the plight of the mentally ill, for their actions were often unpleasant. They seemed so mysterious that they frightened the people around them.

All sorts of things were tried in efforts to rid the sick of the devil. One method was an operation in which an area of the skull was chipped away to form a circular opening so the evil spirits could escape through the hole. Imagine the pain this operation caused, for no one knew about anesthesia in those days. The troubled person was supposed to feel better after the devil left, but infection or other physical problems caused by the operation might have resulted in death or severe disability.

Another popular practice thought to rid a person of the devil was bleeding some blood from the person's body. Leeches—which are bloodsucking worms—were placed on the skin and allowed to suck blood. Purging by laxatives and vomiting from swallowing certain drugs were also used to chase evil spirits. Prayers, flogging, and starvation were some other common ways to make the body uncomfortable so the devil would leave it.

In one report of a doctor trying to cure a mentally ill woman, he was said to have bled her, made her vomit, bled her again, shaved off her hair, rubbed a drug on her head, given her drugs to make her sleep, and bathed her every few hours in warm water in which herbs were dissolved. This was one of the gentler methods of treatment. Many treatments were harsh and seem very cruel today, but they were based on the beliefs of the time. In many cases, treatments were sincere attempts to help troubled people. Sometimes, however, the ill were objects of amusement and torture.

By the end of the fifteenth century, mentally ill people in Europe were commonly believed to be witches. Many were burned alive, strangled, beheaded, or mutilated. In Treges, France, about 7,000 people were burned as witches in a period of several years. One sixteenth-century historian reported that the flames from the execution of witches made Germany red all over.

The mentally ill who were abandoned were left to wander about and beg for food. Many of them were cast adrift on ships in the open sea or auctioned to the bidder who would offer to care for them at the lowest cost to the public. There were monasteries that housed as many mentally disordered people as they could. God's power was called upon to chase the devil from the sick through prayers and religious ceremonies. Faith healing did help some of the sick, but relatively few people were fortunate enough to be cared for this way.

Through the years, many mentally ill were fastened to the floors of dungeons by chains on one hand and one leg. The conditions in which they lived were dark and dirty, and they were often subjected to brutality. Large numbers of people who behaved in odd and disturbing ways were locked away by their families in cellars and attics or placed in homes for the insane that were known as asylums.

Few of these old methods were of much help to those who suffered from mental illness; they usually made things worse. However, they were the only way people knew of to deal with those who were mentally ill. What could be done for a woman who ran up and down the streets of the town, tearing off her clothes and striking everyone? What could be done for a child who could not

Sometimes the mentally ill were left naked and helpless in empty dungeons. *Courtesy of the New York Public Library Picture Collection.*

stop swearing or twitching? How could one deal with a man whose violent actions made him a danger to those around him? Many of the methods that seem cruel today were the result of fear on the part of families and neighbors of the sick.

Through the years there were some understanding voices raised in defense of the mentally ill, but many of them were ignored. This was true as far back as the third or fourth century B.C., when Hippocrates, a Greek physician who is called the father of modern medicine, stated his belief that mental illness results mainly from brain injury or disease. But he could do little to help those who suffered.

In the thirteenth century, the town of Gheel in Belgium became a haven for the mentally ill. According to legend, Dympna, the daughter of an

18

Irish king, fled to Gheel after her father—who was reportedly mad with grief at the death of his wife—proposed marriage to his daughter. According to legend, Dympna was beheaded there by her insane father while the devil looked happily on. After that, some mentally ill were reported to have been healed in Gheel, and Dympna became their patron saint. The townspeople of Gheel began the tradition of caring for the mentally ill, and they continue to do so.

In the sixteenth century, a German physician, Johannes Weyer (1515–88), went against the trend of believing that the mentally ill were witches and claimed that many of them were actually sick. He has been called the first psychiatrist, and he became famous for his kindness to troubled individuals at a time when there was little sympathy for them.

In 1547, the London monastery of St. Mary of Bethlehem became the city hospital where mentally ill patients were chained among the criminals. This hospital, which became known as Bedlam, was famous for the bleeding, baths, and physical restraints used on people who were called mad. The sick were on view to the public, who stared at them after paying a fee to the superintendent of the hospital. The word *bedlam* is still used to describe confusing, noisy situations.

In France, after the Revolution of 1789, Dr.

The padded cell was seen as the "safest" method of keeping the mentally ill confined but was really a way to avoid more costly care. *Courtesy of the New York Public Library Picture Collection.*

Phillipe Pinel was appointed director of an asylum. He ordered that the sick be freed from their chains and allowed fresh air and exercise. Many people feared that the mentally ill would become violent if they were released from their chains, but most became calmer and some recovered. Pinel's action led to a more humane approach to the care for the mentally ill throughout France.

Whereas some doctors held the idea that mental illness might be due partly to physical diseases, others emphasized the importance of family influences, bad habits in ways of thinking, and mistaken beliefs. Their many theories led to a wide variety of treatments for the mentally ill. Toward the end of the nineteenth century, Sigmund Freud played a major role in the development of therapies to help the mentally ill. His theories about how the mind works continue to have a major influence on doctors and other caregivers today. He thought that symptoms of mental disturbance were caused by thoughts and impulses that were hidden away in a part of the mind called the unconscious. He developed ways of bringing these thoughts and feelings into the person's awareness. This technique, called *psychoanalysis,* is still used.

One of the great reform movements that was meant to improve conditions for the mentally ill in the United States was begun by Dorothea Dix, a Massachusetts schoolteacher, in 1840. She begged Congress to help the "insane . . . bound with galling chains, bowed beneath fetters, lacerated with ropes." She had seen disturbed people impris-

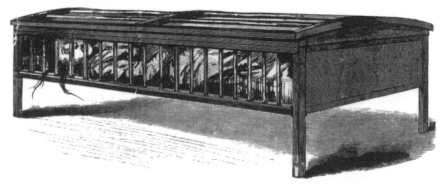

A mentally ill woman was confined to this criblike bed in a New York State institution in 1882. *Courtesy of the New York Public Library Picture Collection.*

oned with criminals, unclothed, and in dark, cold, unsanitary conditions. She confronted the Massachusetts legislature with the inhumane conditions and succeeded in bringing about major reforms.

The treatment of the mentally ill improved over the next fifty years. People were no longer bound by chains, but they still suffered beyond imagination. They were transferred from small communities of mentally ill patients to large state-run fortresslike mental hospitals, where they were supposed to be treated humanely.

By the late nineteenth century and early twentieth century, vast state mental hospitals housed many thousands of the most seriously disturbed people in the United States. Although care was supposed to be better than before, crowded conditions and shortages of funds and trained caregivers meant that many of the patients received little more than food and water. In some parts of the hospitals, large numbers of the mentally ill were locked together in huge rooms without much, or any, medical care. Many people who were less seriously ill but had no one to care for them at home were mixed together with the seriously ill who were living in worlds of their own. Hundreds of naked mental patients were herded into these filthy, barnlike wards. Beds were jammed close together, and many sick people were strapped down or wore straitjackets, which wrapped around their bodies and arms so that they could not move freely.

How could the people who ran the hospitals be so cruel? Actually, in many cases their tasks were overwhelming. Imagine yourself in charge of sixty people. Some of them are quiet, moving only when someone moves them. Many of them are very active, behaving like young children with temper tantrums. Some are wild. They tear off their clothes, are too confused to use the bathroom and soil themselves, break windows, and even gouge pieces out of the walls. Such a scene was typical of what happened in many mental hospitals a few decades ago. Many of the caretakers did the

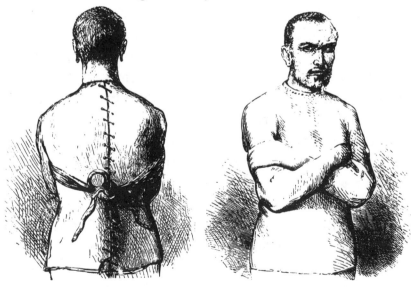

The excuse for the straitjacket was that it would keep the mentally ill from harming themselves. *Courtesy of the New York Public Library Picture Collection.*

best they could to help their patients, but some staff members did not really care what happened, and some seemed to take pleasure in making life worse for the mentally ill. Life in the mental hospitals was often so bad that it made people worse than when they had entered. It tended to create the kind of behavior that is associated with mental illness.

Clifford Beers, a graduate of Yale University, wrote a moving book about his own experiences as a patient in three different mental hospitals. As a result of pressure from readers of this book, *A Mind That Found Itself*, and the support of psychologists such as William James and Adolf Meyer, there was a large movement throughout the United States to educate people about the plight of the mentally ill. This led to the formation of various groups and eventually to the National Association of Mental Health, an organization that is still active in helping to make conditions better for the mentally ill.

During World War II, a large number of men who refused to serve in the armed forces for religious reasons worked in mental hospitals. These conscientious objectors, as they were known, played a big part in exposing some of the terrible conditions they found in the hospitals. According to one report by a conscientious objector, he was taken to a room where he saw 250 men, most of them naked. Some men were standing around the walls of the room. There was no furniture, so those who were seated sat on the floor and on window seats. Some were huddled in corners, but others were wandering around the room picking up excrement and playing with it.

Conditions in a mental hospital were described in a novel called *The Snake Pit* that was published in 1946 by Mary Jane Ward, who was said to have been a nurse in a mental hospital. This and other books helped to make the public conscious of the state hospitals as dumping grounds for the mentally ill. They were being called a place to store people who were troublesome and who had the unfortunate habit of acting crazy. They were thought of as a hiding place for the less attractive members of the community.

In the years following World War II, the public and politicians became much more aware of the extent of mental disease in the United States. Veterans Administration hospitals were said to have 60 percent of their beds filled with mentally ill, and they filled 50 percent of the beds in other hospitals. In 1945, President Harry Truman announced that, although accurate statistics were lacking, at least two million persons in the United States were mentally ill, and as many as ten million would need hospitalization for mental illness in their lifetime.

Now the emphasis was placed on mental health

and the prevention of mental illness. The National Institute of Mental Health was formed. The institute was set up to research the causes and treatment of mental illness, to train more doctors and other mental health experts, and to help states improve their service to the mentally ill.

In the 1950s, the discovery that new medicines, called tranquilizers, could calm the mentally ill played a part in the release of many patients from the large state hospitals. At the same time, there was a movement to reduce the number of patients there because the conditions were so terrible. During the 1960s and 1970s, many abuses were exposed. One observer wrote that the grass on the grounds of the state hospitals received better attention than the patients.

State officials found that there were many people in the hospitals who were no longer in need of care there. They could live in the community and be helped by mental health clinics near them.

Thousands of mental patients were discharged from the hospitals with prescriptions for what many called miracle drugs. But the drugs did not always work as well as doctors and drug companies thought they would. When the sick were away from the hospitals, many of them did not take their medicine according to directions.

During the 1960s and 1970s, many of the people who left the hospitals lived in boardinghouses and inexpensive hotels that had single rooms where occupants could manage to live on income from welfare. When many of these hotels were improved to house middle-class people and the government reduced the funding for the mentally disabled, many of them became homeless.

Only a small percentage of the group homes that were promised as homes for the discharged mentally ill were made available. Community mental health centers could not deal with all the patients who needed help. Many of the mentally ill had no place to go.

3.

Nowhere to Go

The problems of the mentally ill and those who care for them did not go away when large numbers of people left the state hospitals. Many thousands of former patients found places to live with families, in cheap boardinghouses, and in hotels. But when inexpensive housing became scarce in the 1980s, many of the mentally ill moved to the streets. They joined the growing number of people who were not sick but who could no longer pay their rent.

By the time the ranks of homeless swelled, large numbers of discharged mental patients were not getting the treatment they needed at clinics. Ellie was typical of the mentally ill who left a state hospital in the 1970s with a prescription for medicine and instructions to visit a local clinic. She was twenty years old when she left the hospital and moved home. Her parents and two sisters welcomed her warmly, even though they vividly remembered the problems she had caused before she was hospitalized. Ellie suffered from a disorder called *schizophrenia,* and she appeared odd and different. She could not stop herself from making loud noises for no apparent reason.

Ellie's habit of making strange hooting sounds and talking to someone who was not there bothered her family when she came back to live with them, but they knew she could not control this. They tried to ignore her strange behavior and the unpleasant noises that she made frequently.

During the next two weeks, Ellie kept the two appointments that were made with the social worker at a mental health clinic near her family's home. When she went to the clinic the first time, she had to sit in the waiting room for two hours. Ellie was under great stress, and the hooting noises came frequently. She had no control over them, but the other patients in the waiting room moved as far away from her as they could. Finally, Ellie was invited into the office of a man who said he was going to help her. He asked so many questions that Ellie wanted to run out of the room.

At the prodding of her sisters, Ellie went back for a second visit to the clinic. This time she did not have to wait long, and she rather enjoyed talking to the social worker. But she hated the walk to reach the clinic, and she missed her next two appointments. The clinic secretary made a few attempts to reach Ellie by phone and mail, but after that Ellie's name was dropped from the list of patients at the clinic.

During the next few years, Ellie's sisters found her strange behavior very annoying. They nagged her about her odd habits and complained that they could no longer bring their friends home because they were ashamed of having a "crazy" sister. To make matters worse, Ellie's parents "bugged her" about taking her medicine. Even when she did take it, she had trouble controlling the hooting. Home was not as pleasant as it was when she first returned.

Ellie was still in touch with a woman she had known at the hospital, so she left home to live with this friend at an old house near the hospital. She went home to pick up her government check each month, and she gave it to her friend. Together, they bought food and medicine, and they paid some of the bills for the house.

Living together was good for Ellie and her friend until the friend began to hear voices that told her not to clean the house. She thought there were evil spirits hiding in the house who did not want to be disturbed. So the garbage piled up, and the house smelled so awful that neighbors called the health department, which closed the house.

Ellie and her friend moved to the old railroad tracks where a group of homeless people lived. She still stopped home for her government check each month, but she ignored the pleas of her family to move back with them. Ellie would spend the rest of her life among the homeless.

Many of the seriously mentally ill who left the mental hospitals in the last few decades have wound up on the streets and in shelters. Fifteen-year-old Gina left the hospital six months ago in a cotton dress which she wore for the next two months. She made her home in a shed behind a boardinghouse. Neighbors, who knew she was there, left food in bags at her door, but they knew better than to wait for her to greet them. She swore and threw the bags of food at anyone who came near her. She was in a rage much of the time. After two months, Gina's neighbors called the Department of Social Services, and she was returned to the hospital for a few months. Since then, she has been in and out of the hospital four times.

When Gina goes to the hospital, which was her home for many years, she stays only a few days. When she is there, she gets a bath, some regular meals, and some medicine. She takes the medicine while she is in the hospital, but when she leaves, she sells it, unless someone steals it from her first.

Gina now lives in a shelter some of the time, but she prefers to be on the street. She complains that people steal her things at the shelter. The "things" are an assortment of items she has collected from various trash bins, but they are important to her. Now and then, she finds empty soda bottles and cans in trash containers, and she manages to redeem them for enough money to buy some chocolate candy. Gina is one of a large number of individuals who spend years of their lives among the homeless.

How many of the homeless are mentally ill? This is a question without an answer, but estimates vary from 25 percent to 35 percent. Some of this group consists of people who were released from mental hospitals during the past several decades with little or no follow-up.

There are so many individuals like Ellie and Gina on the streets that some people think all of the mentally ill should be kept locked up in hospitals. Many of them appear weird, but are they dangerous? Do they have a right to live on the streets if they are not harming themselves or others?

Back in the days when no one paid any attention to the rights of the mentally ill, a person could be committed to an institution simply because he or she was "mentally ill and in need of treatment." Some patients should never have been committed in the first place.

After the activists of the 1960s and 1970s began comparing mental patients to blacks, who were denied civil rights, the Supreme Court took action. It ruled in 1975 that people could not be committed to institutions against their will and kept locked up indefinitely simply because of mental illness. From then on, proof of dangerousness to themselves and/or others was required for commitment. The courts also said that mental patients have the right to the least restrictive treatment program, which meant they should be treated in the community if possible.

Before this, nobody worried about what mentally ill people needed after they left the hospital because most people never left. But when the laws changed and thousands of people were discharged from institutions, other kinds of problems sprang up. Some former patients ended up in jails, on the streets, or in nursing homes where conditions were even worse than in the mental hospitals. The mental health system lost track of hundreds of thousands of discharged mental patients. It became clear that the mental health clinics and other facilities in the community were inadequate to track and treat the huge numbers of people who needed follow-up help.

Not everyone who is discharged from a mental hospital stays troubled or becomes homeless. Some people are able to live on their own and are conscientious about keeping clinic appointments for medication. Others live with their families, who make sure they get help. The big problem lies with the mentally ill people who do not have the support they need. If there is no system in place to keep track of these people after they leave the hospital, they are very likely to get worse. Some states have good aftercare programs, but in other states, follow-up is haphazard.

The quality of mental health care varies from state to state, but many ex-patients are fortunate to live in communities where they can find some measure of freedom and dignity. Stamford, Connecticut, is one of these places.

St. Luke's Community Services in Stamford is a model of support for some of the physically or psychologically challenged. If you were mentally ill and lucky enough to become a resident at St. Luke's, you could live in a building that was once the YWCA. Residents include formerly homeless families of two parents and children, single women and children, individuals with mental disorders, and people with AIDS. A variety of human services would help you to move toward independent living. You would help to cook the meals, attend a training program that would prepare you for a job, take your medicine under supervision each day, but be free to come and go as you please. But there aren't enough places with the quality of support found at St. Luke's.

Four programs serve over 1,000 people in New York City, where there are an estimated 95,000 seriously mentally ill people. About 8,500 of them are homeless. Project Help is an example of a program in New York City in which a team of professional caregivers cruise the city in a van to check on the homeless who are seriously mentally ill. They persuade some of them to enter places such as Fountain House, a model social agency that cares for people with emotional problems. One resident of Fountain House praises the people who work there because they treat her with respect. "They don't talk down to you like a sickie," she says. Her life is much better than in the days when they put people in "what they called the nuthouse."

In many states, large numbers of people live in group homes and supervised apartments, where they make much greater progress than in the huge mental hospitals that once cared for the mentally ill. In these community programs, residents are monitored and the taking of medicine is supervised.

Unfortunately, there are not enough places for those who want to be part of these programs. There are many self-help groups and organizations like NAMI, which has state and local branches that provide support and help to improve the quality of life for the mentally ill and their families, but they can only help a small percentage of those who need a place to live.

Not every mentally ill person who lives on the streets wants another place to live. One of the most famous cases of a troubled homeless person who refused treatment time after time is that of Larry Hogue. This man terrorized a neighborhood in Manhattan's Upper West Side for years by threatening people with knives, using foul language, and holding newspapers that were burning like torches while approaching men and women who walked along the street. Larry Hogue's problems with drug addiction and mental illness put him in and out of jails over a period of years.

Should Larry Hogue and others like him be in jail or in the hospital? While some people need to be confined because they are dangerous to the community or themselves, mentally ill people are often jailed because of relatively trivial charges or on account of behavior that is the result of their illness. Many jails do not provide adequate service for mentally ill inmates. Only one out of five jails has access to mental health services, and most corrections officers receive little or no training in dealing with the problems of the mentally ill. After they leave jail, only about one-third of released inmates receive treatment for their mental illness.

Even some large prisons that have mental health facilities and psychiatrists to care for the mentally ill inmates are shamefully inadequate. At one large prison in upstate New York, a class-action lawsuit was filed on behalf of mentally ill prisoners who were locked in solitary cells containing only a bare mattress by corrections officers, without treatment, and in some cases without being seen by a psychiatrist for several days. Other prisoners who were not mentally ill were locked in the isolation cells of the psychiatric facility because of disruptive behavior.

More supervision by state and federal authorities is needed in order to ensure basic rights and humane treatment for the mentally ill in prisons and jails. Corrections officers should receive training regarding mental illness. Prisoners should have access to psychiatric services. The National Alliance for the Mentally Ill has been active in pursuing reforms.

Many people do not care whether the mentally ill are in jail or in mental hospitals; they think all these people should be locked away. But the vast majority of mentally ill people are not dangerous, and only 2 percent of former mental patients pose any danger to others. (By contrast, some of the most dangerous people in our society are drunk drivers, who account for about half of all fatal automobile accidents.) Although there has been an increase in arrests of former mental patients, this increase is only among people who had arrest records before they were hospitalized. Despite the evidence to the contrary, a survey done in California found that 83 percent of the people polled thought that mental patients were dangerous.

Who is to blame for these wrong ideas? Many

NAMI's Programs
for Families

• *Advocacy for services.* At federal, state, and local levels, NAMI demands improved services for people with severe mental illnesses, such as greater access to treatment, housing, and employment, and better health insurance.

• *Support.* Local self-help support groups enable members to share concerns, learn about mental illnesses, and receive practical advice on treatment and community resources. Special interest networks offer additional support regarding children and adolescents, consumers (patients), culture and language concerns, curriculum and training (for professionals), forensic issues, guardianships and trusts, the homeless and missing, religious outreach, siblings and adult children, and veterans.

• *Education.* NAMI provides up-to-date, scientific information through publications, a toll-free helpline (1-800-950-NAMI), and annual Mental Illness Awareness Week campaign.

• *Support for research.* NAMI actively supports increased federal and private funding for research into causes and treatments of severe mental illness.

Source: National Alliance for the Mentally Ill.

people blame the newspapers and television; violent crimes committed by mentally ill individuals are highly publicized and sensationalized. These cases always focus attention on the so-called insanity defense. *Insanity* is a legal term, not a medical term. An accused person may be found "not guilty by reason of insanity" if it is determined that he or she was not capable of understanding that he or she was doing something wrong at the time of the crime. Some people think the insanity defense is

41

abused, but the reality is that it is invoked in only about 1 of every 1,000 cases. Many people are afraid that the individual may be discharged after only a short time in a psychiatric institution, but this is rarely the case when a violent crime has been committed. John W. Hinckley, Jr., who attempted to assassinate President Ronald Reagan in 1981, was found not guilty by reason of insanity and was committed to a mental institution. He was still confined to the psychiatric hospital fifteen years later. In Hinckley's case, there was much disagreement among the expert witnesses as to whether he was really insane.

But the mentally ill individuals who commit violent acts are rare. Former mental patients almost always act like everyone else. You can help stop the stigma by spreading the truth.

4.

The Many Faces of Mental Illness

Your heart pounds. You can't breathe. You have a terrible feeling that something horrible is going to happen, and you cannot control it. You think you are going "crazy." Now you feel as if you are going to die. You are about to have a panic attack.

Medical tests show that there is nothing physically wrong with you, but what happens is very real. Some people have just one panic attack and never have another. Others suffer many attacks. These people suffer from *panic disorder,* an illness that affects 1.6 percent of the population in the United States. Panic disorder can start at any age, but most often it begins in young adults.

When *panic attacks* come back again and again, as is often the case, the person may begin to feel anxious all the time, fearful that another panic attack may strike. People sometimes develop irrational fears, known as *phobias,* about situations where an attack has occurred. Robin experienced a panic attack that came out of the blue while she was shopping in the local mall. Two weeks later, when her mother asked her to do some shopping, she became very anxious about returning to the mall and refused to go because she was so fearful. About one-third of people with panic disorder develop a condition called *agoraphobia*, or fear of being away from home. People with agoraphobia often feel safer if a family member or friend accompanies them when they go out, but if they are too fearful to leave their homes to work or attend school, this condition can keep them from leading a normal life.

Some people have phobias that make them uncomfortable, but which do not hamper their lives as much as agoraphobia. Fear of heights, elevators, or snakes are examples of some of these phobias.

Relief from anxiety is available; treatment with new medications and behavior therapy can help most people who suffer from panic disorder or phobias. Behavior therapy helps people face the things they fear by gradually exposing them to the situations that trigger the fear. With help and support, they are able to conquer their anxiety, often within two or three months.

Obsessive-compulsive disorder (OCD) is another condition that causes anxiety and interferes with a person's life. It was considered rare at one time, but now it is believed to affect about 2 to 3 percent of the population. Jan's mother has OCD. She was always unusually fussy, and living with her was

Rebecca, the eighteen-year-old artist of this self-portrait, has been diagnosed with emotional problems. She enjoys art because she is able to express her feelings and ease her mind.

very difficult. She used Scotch tape to remove specks of dirt from the carpets; she scrubbed her shoes; she washed her keys. She kept the clothing in her closet in a special order and made certain that each piece of clothing was always in its proper place. She insisted that Jan wash her hands at least a dozen times each day in order to be free of germs. As for her own germs, Jan's mother took six showers daily.

Obsessions are unwanted ideas that repeatedly well up in the mind of a person with OCD. They cannot be explained and are inconvenient, often frightening, and sometimes bizarre. Obsessions cause anxiety. To reduce their anxiety, people may develop *compulsions,* which are ritual acts that are repeated again and again. For example, someone obsessed by doubts about an unlocked door may keep checking the lock.

Typical compulsions are excessive housecleaning, hand washing, and repeated actions such as counting, touching, arranging, and hoarding. Compulsion has been described as a "hiccup in the brain." The people who suffer from obsessions and compulsions know that their fears and behaviors do not make sense, but they cannot control having them. For example, Jan's mother knows that the time she spends washing and cleaning could be spent in more pleasant ways, but she cannot stop herself. The disorder seems to have taken over her life, and it has a serious effect on her whole family.

Medication and behavior therapy can help people with OCD, so that they no longer feel compelled to carry out their rituals. For example, a boy who could not go through a doorway without touching the right side of the door and turning around five times was helped to give up his ritual by a therapist. He eventually developed the courage to go through the doorway in a normal way. Imagine what a relief this was to him and his family.

While people who have OCD are usually aware that they have a problem, many girls and young adults who have eating disorders deny them. Eating disorders are most common in adolescent girls, although they do occur in older women and in men. As many as 1 percent of young girls suffer from *anorexia nervosa,* a dangerous condition in which they literally starve themselves, sometimes to death.

Parents and friends often do not realize at first that there is anything wrong with the person who has anorexia. Paul's older sister, Becky, felt that she was not good at anything and that her body was not attractive. She was obsessed with the thought that she was too fat. By eating very little, she could control a part of her life. Strict dieting and exercising every day made her feel good. At first, there were many compliments, but later she looked so thin, people were always asking her if she was trying to starve herself to death. Paul was tired of listening to their parents beg his sister to eat. He complained that no one cared about what he ate and that all the meals were planned around what Becky liked so that she would gain some weight.

Becky avoided big scenes at mealtime by eating alone. She wore dresses around the house that made her look heavier than she really was so that her parents would not fuss about how thin she was getting. She was not concerned about reports that anorexia could affect her health in serious ways. She did not believe the reports that said extreme dieting could cause damage to important organs such as the brain and heart. She did notice that her nails were brittle and her skin was becoming yellow and dry. She did not believe the doctor who told her that losing so much weight could make her brain shrink and cause personality problems. But she did notice that she felt tired and irritable most of the time, and she no longer enjoyed going out with her friends.

Becky's doctor gave her pamphlets about the seriousness of anorexia. Her whole family, including Paul, who had always been jealous of the attention she received, helped her understand her illness and encouraged her to get help. She needed lots of understanding and encouragement to stay in the treatment program, but she did succeed in overcoming her illness.

About 2 to 3 percent of young girls in the United States suffer from *bulimia,* a pattern of eating large amounts of food and then ridding their bodies of excess calories by vomiting, taking enemas, and/or abusing laxatives. Some follow strict exercise routines to avoid gaining weight. They "binge and purge" in secret to maintain their normal body weight.

Cindy ate huge amounts of food, but she did not gain weight because she forced herself to vomit. She hated herself for doing this, but when things were not going well, she craved food. She felt unable to control herself and would eat pounds of cake and candy at one time, then make herself vomit. She found this routine disgusting, and she did not tell anyone because she was too embarrassed. She felt anxious, frightened, and depressed, and her throat was becoming raw from the stomach acid that bathed it when she vomited. After she tried to commit suicide, she was taken to the hospital. There she was able to talk about some of the things that made her upset. After she left the hospital, she began attending an eating disorder clinic. Her eating habits were difficult to change, but with the support of family, friends, and her doctor, she stopped the habit that was becoming a serious health problem.

One of the more common kinds of mental disorders among children is *attention deficit/hyperactivity disorder (AD/HD)*. You may know someone who is overly active, inattentive, and/or impulsive. Not everyone with these characteristics has AD/HD, but many do. And those who do have many different symptoms.

This is what happened to Bill. He was an active baby, much to the delight of his parents, but they soon began to wish he would be less active. By the time he was two years old, he would run around the house, open drawers and dump the contents on the floor, pull the towels off the racks, and toss his toys around rather than play with them. He seemed to always be in motion. Bill was a child with attention deficit/hyperactivity disorder.

Through the next few years, Bill continued to dart from one activity to another, leaving a trail of toys behind him. In nursery school, when all the other kids napped after lunch, Bill could not lie still. One teacher was appointed to sit next to Bill in order to keep him on the sleeping mat. On the playground, he seemed no wilder than the other kids. But his tendency to overreact, such as hitting playmates who simply bumped into him, caused trouble for him in the early years of school.

By the time Bill reached middle school, he was diagnosed as having AD/HD and another problem called *conduct disorder* (starting fights, lying, and stealing). His parents struggled to help him as best they could, but when Bill was young, no one knew about medicines that could have helped. His grandparents told them not to worry and said that "boys will be boys." Friends and neighbors blamed the parents for not disciplining Bill, but these people did not know that the usual methods of discipline, such as reasoning and scolding, don't work with a child who suffers from AD/HD. These kids do not choose to act this way. Their self-control comes and goes. Later in life Bill suffered from depression, another illness that is frequently associated with AD/HD.

Today, an expert in mental health would have diagnosed Bill as suffering from AD/HD when he was a toddler. AD/HD is a brain disorder that can be helped by special medicines that act to improve concentration and decrease restlessness. But before a doctor decides what is wrong with a child like Bill, other disorders that might cause similar symptoms must be ruled out. Several conditions can look like AD/HD but are not, so it is important that a professional be consulted about what actions to take.

Not only do children with AD/HD frequently develop other kinds of mental disorders, they often have other disorders at the same time. For example, about one-quarter of the children who have AD/HD also have trouble talking, listening, reading, and writing. This causes problems with learning, even though their intelligence is normal.

A very small proportion of people with AD/HD also have a rare disorder called *Tourette's syndrome*. People with Tourette's have *tics*, a kind of behavior that happens again and again and cannot be controlled. For example, one boy needs to touch his shoes every few minutes. Some people with Tourette's have other movements, like facial twitches or eye blinks, that they cannot control. Some of them make loud noises, swear, or have other kinds of uncontrollable behaviors. At least half of the patients with Tourette's also have AD/HD, but the opposite is not true (half of the kids with AD/HD do not have Tourette's).

Another rare but tragic condition that occurs in children is *autism*. Although it has been mistaken for schizophrenia in children, it is not the same. Autism is a brain disorder that begins before the age of three. Parents often notice something wrong when the child is an infant. These children seem detached, unable to be involved emotionally with those around them. Their ability to speak is very abnormal; some never learn, while others have their own language.

Mark is a five-year-old who does not talk much, but he repeats the same words over and over. His mother describes him as living in a shell. Sometimes he sits on the floor for hours, rocking back and forth. He is not interested in anyone in the room, but he does look at his own hands and other body parts. When his mother gives him a pad of paper and a pencil, he draws circles, one after another. When she tries to hug him, he kicks and screams. He seems to look right through people who try to carry on a conversation with him.

The problems of each autistic child are different from those of every other, but all autistic children seem disconnected to some extent with the outside world. They are unable to interact appropriately with other people, and seem unaware of others' needs or feelings. Many of them like to arrange objects in a certain pattern and to watch shiny or moving objects. About three-quarters of autistic children function at a retarded level. Even those with normal intelligence may have disturbances in language and communication. For instance, a four-year-old may have a good vocabulary, but may have difficulty understanding simple questions. Autistic children depend on rigid routines for a sense of security and may have temper tantrums if anything is changed. Their behavior is always difficult for families to deal with.

Toxic substances such as alcohol, cocaine, amphetamines, PCP (angel dust), poisons, and even medicines prescribed by a physician may affect the brain. Infections, imbalances in body chemistry, liver or kidney disease, some vitamin deficiencies, stroke, head injury, and certain diseases that attack the nervous system can also damage the brain and cause dementia. Dementia is a condition marked by memory loss, inability to learn new information, loss of skills that the individual had previously, inability to plan or deal with new situations, difficulty naming objects and people, and difficulty understanding questions or requests. The person may not know the date or the street, city, or state where he or she lives. He or she may not be able to perform very simple tasks. He or she may not recognize family members and may not even remember his or her own name. In some instances, the dementia is progressive, and the person becomes mute, bedridden, and eventually unable to understand or do anything. This is the case when someone has dementia of the Alzheimer's type. Between 2 and 4 percent of people over 65 years of age are estimated to have *Alzheimer's disease*. No one really knows what causes the abnormalities that are found in the brains of people who have this disease, but scientists are working to find the cause and possible prevention or cure. It is an especially sad condition that is stressful for families who are caretakers. They must watch their loved ones deteriorate, losing their mental abilities slowly over a period of years. Fortunately, help is available in the form of resources such as support groups for families of people with Alzheimer's.

Panic disorder, eating disorders, and other problems mentioned in this chapter are just a small sample of the hundreds of kinds of mental disorders from which many people suffer silently and needlessly. Among the most severe of these illnesses are schizophrenia and depression, which are discussed in the following chapters.

5.

What Is Schizophrenia?

Schizophrenia is one of the most severe kinds of mental illness, and one of the most cruel. There are probably twice as many people with schizophrenia living in shelters and on the streets as there are in public mental hospitals. Today there is hope for the treatment of this brain disease that affects 1 in every 100 Americans during their lifetime.

When more people with schizophrenia reveal that they suffer from this disease, there is less stigma attached to it. In 1995, when Michael B. Laudor revealed that he was schizophrenic, he had graduated from Yale University summa cum laude in three years instead of four and from Yale Law School, where he was a senior editor of the *Yale Law Review*. He is a role model who does not believe that mental illness need stop his career. But many people still refuse to accept the idea that anyone with such a serious disease can accomplish much, in spite of the new drugs that help a person to cope with, and even conquer, this common mental illness. People's attitudes about schizophrenia and other mental illnesses are quite different from those held about a physical disease.

When Maria's father had a heart attack, everyone was very sympathetic and helpful. Friends and family visited him and gave him encouragement when he was feeling upset about being sick. But a year later, when Maria's sister Jodi began doing some odd things, no one knew what to say or how to help her problem.

Although Maria and Jodi were close in age, they had always been very different. Thirteen-year-old Maria was outgoing and enjoyed being with many friends, whereas fifteen-year-old Jodi kept to herself more. This was not especially strange, but then Jodi became even more withdrawn. She found it difficult to concentrate on her schoolwork, and her grades dropped. Near the end of the school year, she began refusing to attend classes, but she would not discuss her problem with the school counselor or with her parents.

Maria thought that Jodi's behavior was very mysterious and scary. When her friends came to the house, Maria tried to keep them away from Jodi, but sometimes Jodi slipped into the room where they were talking and did some bizarre things, like laying her hands on their heads. It was all very embarrassing. Maria's friends stopped visiting because they didn't know what to say or how to act when Jodi was there.

Sometimes Jodi expressed feelings that did not seem to be connected with what was happening; her emotions did not match the situation. For instance, when her mother received a letter telling of the death of an elderly cousin, Jodi showed no sadness on hearing the news but seemed more interested in the pretty writing paper. At other times she burst into tears for no apparent reason.

People with schizophrenia often exhibit inappropriate emotions. Some show very little feeling about anything; they appear bland and do not relate well to other people. They talk with no expression or animation. These individuals are said to have *flat affect*. One young man who complained that he never felt any emotions repeatedly cut himself with a knife in order to hurt himself and see blood. For him, feeling pain was better than feeling nothing.

People with schizophrenia often have conflicting feelings; they don't know how they feel. The term *ambivalence* is often used to describe normal feelings of uncertainty or mixed emotions. But in schizophrenia, contradictory feelings present at the same time may be so strong that the person cannot act on anything. The individual may express love and hatred for another in the same sentence. One day, Jodi told Maria that she loved her dearly but thought she was a mean, horrible

Patients who express themselves visually sometimes build their own reasons for what their pictures mean.

person. Then she hugged Maria and called her a wonderful sister.

Jodi's mother and teachers knew that she was seriously troubled. When her parents realized that she was not "snapping out" of this moody spell, they became very concerned and took her to the family doctor, who referred her to a psychiatrist.

At first, Jodi did not want to discuss anything with the psychiatrist; she was afraid he would say she was crazy and lock her up in a hospital. He asked her a lot of questions about herself: about school, her family, her interests, and what she liked to do in her spare time. He also persuaded her to tell him some of the things that were bothering her. He was sympathetic and patient, and he seemed to understand when she lost her train of thought and couldn't say exactly what she meant. She finally told him about the voices she was hearing. One time, she heard a voice coming from the radio that told her to hide in her bedroom. For the next week, Jodi hardly spoke to Maria or her parents, but she did not explain the reason. No wonder everyone was puzzled and upset by her behavior. They thought that perhaps they were responsible in some way for Jodi's state of mind. Maria began to worry that she might become weird like her sister.

After talking with Jodi, the psychiatrist told her parents that he thought she was showing symptoms of schizophrenia. They became very upset because like most people, they weren't sure exactly what it was. Did Jodi have a "split personality"? There are many false ideas about this disease. (See chapter 8 on myths.) People may not have much empathy for those with schizophrenia because it is difficult to imagine what it might be like to be ruled by bizarre thoughts and behave as though possessed by mysterious forces. The individual with schizophrenia no longer seems like the same person he or she used to be. This appeared to be the case with Jodi.

Dr. Campbell, the psychiatrist, made an appointment to talk with Jodi's family in order to help them understand this scary disease. He explained that it was important for them to learn about schizophrenia if they wanted to help Jodi. He told them that it is a disease of the brain, as real as cancer or pneumonia or her father's heart disease.

Schizophrenia is probably not a single disorder but is more likely a group of similar conditions. Not all people with schizophrenia have exactly the same symptoms. And it may have more than one cause.

Dr. Campbell said that Jodi's brain was playing tricks on her and that she could not help what was happening. She had become supersensitive to the sights and sounds around her, and the constant bombardment was very upsetting. Ordinary items in her room—like the desk, the chair, the curtains on the window, and the books on the shelf—all seemed equally important to her. Most people familiar with the room would not take much notice of these things, but Jodi was finding that all these objects were vying for her attention. The objects also seemed changed in some way. For example, her comfortable old desk chair looked menacing to her, but she could not explain why. She heard children playing outside her window, and each voice seemed to be sending a special message to her. In people with schizophrenia, the brain does not screen out background sights and sounds as it does for other people. In other words, the part of the brain that acts as a filter does not work properly. This makes it very difficult for people like Jodi to concentrate on a train of thought or to pay attention to one thing.

Many people with schizophrenia are bombarded with a flood of inner thoughts, feelings, and memories, as well as sensations from outside. One patient in the state mental hospital did not like taking his medicine because, he complained, it allowed him to have only one or two thoughts in his head at a time. Without the medicine, he could hold at least a dozen thoughts in his mind at once. This was a pleasant state for him, but for Jodi, it was so distracting that she could not concentrate on her schoolwork or carry on a coherent conversation. Other people with schizophrenia may suffer from poverty of thought; that is, they seem to have fewer thoughts than normal people.

Because there is a defect in the way the brain

Mental illness can occur at any age. The artist of this picture is a thirteen-year-old boy who is considered violent.

sorts out and interprets information, thinking is confused in individuals with schizophrenia. In some people with this disease, logical links between one thought and the next may be only slightly disconnected, but in others, speech is so disorganized and disconnected that it makes little or no sense to anyone listening. *Word salad* is a term applied to extremely jumbled speech. In a letter to his psychiatrist, a man wrote, "same slave bond through film actors . . . faith circulars only to here from Mary Reen."

Schizophrenia made Jodi lose the ability to think logically. For example, Dr. Campbell asked her what she would do if she found a stamped, addressed, and sealed envelope on the street. You

66

might say you would put it in the nearest mailbox. Jodi said she would take it home and save it carefully until the owner claimed it.

Jodi noticed another strange thing happening to her. She sometimes was not sure where her body ended and the rest of the world began. Her hands looked foreign to her, as though they belonged to someone else. Alterations in the sense of one's self are not uncommon in schizophrenia. One young girl confused herself with a doll and thought that she would be in the doll's cradle if her mother placed the doll there.

It is not unusual for people with schizophrenia to hear voices, as Jodi did, or experience other sensations that have not been stimulated by real cues. These are called *hallucinations.* The most common kinds in schizophrenia are auditory (hearing voices, music, or other sounds). But hallucinations can also be visual (seeing people, animals, or objects), tactile (feeling sensations, often unpleasant, like snakes in the belly), or olfactory (smelling nonexistent odors).

Jodi did not realize that Maria's friends thought her behavior was odd when she laid her hands on their heads. She did this because she believed she had the power to protect them from harm. This belief was a *delusion,* a firmly held conviction without any basis in reality. Many people with schizophrenia have delusions. Some are *paranoid delusions,* false beliefs that people are watching them or planning to harm them. A common one is that the person is being watched by the FBI or CIA. Sometimes delusional individuals think they are wired and that their thoughts are being monitored and broadcast. Others believe thoughts are being inserted into their heads.

Hallucinations and delusions are related to the disorder of thinking, misinterpretation of things that are seen and heard, and faulty processing of information. Jodi's family made a common mistake by trying to convince her that her perceptions and beliefs were incorrect. Their efforts were useless and only made Jodi feel upset and angry.

Behavior that seems very bizarre or even frightening to other people seems perfectly logical to a person with schizophrenia. For instance, Gary's voices tell him he must stand very quietly with his arms outstretched and his eyes closed—otherwise a great earthquake will destroy the city. To Gary, it makes sense to obey the voices and prevent a disaster.

Janet was a young woman who was discovered by a police officer in an alley in Boston. She was sitting in a very uncomfortable-looking contorted position with her arms stuck out at odd angles. She did not stir, and she stared straight ahead without blinking. When the officer asked, "What's wrong?" Janet answered, "What's wrong?" He asked for her name, and she replied, "Name." This repetition of other people's words is known as *echolalia.*

Janet's bizarre condition is *catatonia.* It is sometimes seen in people with schizophrenia, but it may also be a feature of mood disorders, brain diseases, or drug intoxication. People with catatonia may show a variety of symptoms, such as excitement, stupor, grimacing, or immobility. Some have echolalia, like Janet, whereas others are mute. Some imitate other people's actions or posture; this is called *echopraxia.* Occasionally, an individual with catatonia manifests another dramatic symptom called *waxy flexibility.* When the person's arms or legs are moved, they remain in the position to which they were moved.

Catatonia is one of the more dramatic and rare conditions associated with schizophrenia. More commonly, people with schizophrenia show a wide variety of symptoms that are not so obvious, especially in the early stages of the illness. Friends and relatives often feel puzzled, confused, angry, frightened, or guilty. Jodi's family and friends were no exception, and they had many concerns to discuss with the psychiatrist.

6.

Diagnosis and Treatment of Mental Illness

Jodi's family had many questions about her illness when they learned it was schizophrenia. What caused it? Could it have been prevented? Will she ever recover? Will she spend the rest of her life in and out of hospitals? Will she become violent or suicidal? What is the best treatment? How can the family help?

Some people consider a diagnosis of schizophrenia worse than a death sentence. One mother said she wished her daughter had leukemia instead of schizophrenia because she would have a better chance of recovery. Jodi's parents felt the same way, and they had hoped that tests would show she had some other disease.

Jodi's psychiatrist, Dr. Campbell, had told her family that there are several conditions that can mimic schizophrenia. Brain tumors or viral encephalitis (a disease caused by a virus that infects the brain) may produce symptoms that are like those of schizophrenia. Street drugs such as LSD, PCP (angel dust), amphetamines (speed), marijuana, and even some prescription drugs can all cause symptoms that look like schizophrenia.

Jodi went to the hospital for a physical examination and tests. The doctor there asked her and her parents many questions about her medical history, including illnesses and injuries in the past, recent physical problems, and about any medicines or drugs she took. The doctor said that Jodi did not have an infection and that her symptoms were not caused by drugs. A special test called an *encephalogram,* or *EEG,* was done; this is a harmless procedure for measuring electrical impulses in the brain, so-called brainwaves. She also had another risk-free and painless test known as *magnetic resonance imaging,* or *MRI,* which allows doctors to see the structure of any part of the body in great detail. The results of these tests showed that Jodi did not have a brain tumor.

In many people with schizophrenia, abnormalities are found in specific parts of the brain. Special tests often reveal subtle differences such as slowed reaction time and unusual eye movements. Researchers have also found that the brains of schizophrenics differ from healthy brains in the way the blood flows and in the way the brain uses oxygen and glucose (a form of sugar) in certain areas.

There is no special laboratory test that can identify schizophrenia, and nobody really knows with certainty what causes it. Dr. Campbell told

Jodi's parents that they did not cause her illness, nor could they have prevented it. A combination of factors may have been responsible.

In Jodi's case, no one in the family was known to have had a serious mental illness, but studies have shown that schizophrenia often runs in families. If one parent has schizophrenia, a child's risk of developing schizophrenia is ten times greater than that of the general population. If both parents have schizophrenia, the child has a 35 to 45 percent chance of getting schizophrenia, compared with only a 1 percent risk if neither parent has schizophrenia. If one of a pair of identical twins has schizophrenia, the other is affected in a high percentage of cases, between 33 and 78 percent. Fraternal twins have a lower rate, about the same as for other brothers and sisters. Studies of adopted children have also helped demonstrate that a hereditary factor is important. But there must be something else at work; otherwise all identical twins would have the disease when one of them does. Something in the environment may trigger the disease in someone who has the hereditary tendency.

People who are born during the winter months are more likely to develop schizophrenia than those born at other times of the year. No one knows why, but this finding suggests that something is going on very early, perhaps a seasonal occurrence during conception or pregnancy, that makes the individual susceptible to schizophrenia later in life.

One theory is that some kind of a virus that remains quiet for years before it affects the body may be involved. Certain viruses, known as *retroviruses*, can invade the body cells and remain hidden indefinitely. Infection of brain cells by a retrovirus early in life could cause damage that shows up years later as schizophrenia.

Some researchers suggest that a virus might trigger the production of substances that may damage brain tissue directly. The substances may also interfere with the brain chemicals that carry the messages from one end of a nerve cell to the end of a nearby branch of another nerve cell. These chemicals are called *neurotransmitters*. The most widely accepted theory of schizophrenia is that there is a disturbance in the action of the neurotransmitter known as *dopamine*. It is known that certain drugs that are effective in treating the symptoms of schizophrenia interfere with the action of dopamine. Other drugs, such as amphetamines, which increase the amount of dopamine in the brain, can produce symptoms that are like those of schizophrenia. Dopamine is only one of many substances involved in the functioning of the nervous system. Researchers are continuing to investigate this complicated network of chemicals in order to determine their role in schizophrenia. Such studies can tell scientists what the problem is, but not how it came to be.

Learning about all these theories concerning the possible causes of schizophrenia came as only a small relief for Jodi's family. They were glad to know that they were not the cause of her illness, but they wondered whether stress might have caused it. The family had moved from another state a year earlier, and Jodi had been unhappy about leaving her school and friends. Many people think that overwork, family problems, or other life stresses can cause schizophrenia. It is known that severe stress can sometimes cause symptoms that look like schizophrenia. But stress affects everyone in different ways; what is stressful to one person may be challenging to another.

There is no clear evidence that stress causes schizophrenia. If this were the case, there should have been a high incidence of schizophrenia in the Nazi concentration camps, and among soldiers during World War II. Yet the rate is high in some places that have always been peaceful.

Stress may be a trigger in someone who is already vulnerable to schizophrenia. Schizophrenia generally strikes people between the ages of fifteen and twenty-five, a time of life when there are always many changes and stressful events. No one could be sure that the stress of moving had triggered

Some patients who use art therapy to help them deal with their illness may also demonstrate artistic ability.

Jodi's illness. There was no guarantee that remaining in their former home would have prevented it.

Studies that follow people with schizophrenia for years show that 25 percent recover completely, usually within the first two years. Twenty-five percent are greatly improved, and another 25 percent are somewhat improved. The other 25 percent do not improve. Of this last group, the risk of depression and suicide is high, mostly because of the pain and hopelessness their illness causes them. Ten percent of people with schizophrenia will have committed suicide after ten years, and after thirty years, 15 percent will be dead from suicide. It is difficult to predict what will happen in Jodi's case, but her parents were reassured to know that there is hope of improvement.

Schizophrenia has long been such a mystery that little could be done to help patients in the past. Although there is no cure for schizophrenia, there is treatment. The most important treatment is the use of medicines called *antipsychotic* (or *neuroleptic*) *drugs*, which control the symptoms of schizophrenia. These drugs have also been called tranquilizers, but they should not be. Their purpose is not to tranquilize, although this is a side effect of some drugs. They work by acting on nerve cells that use dopamine and other neurotransmitters in the brain, as mentioned earlier. They reduce delusions (false beliefs such as "I am the King of England")

and hallucinations (hearing sounds, and feeling, smelling, or seeing things that are not there) and can help clear up confused thinking. The antipsychotic drugs produce improvement in about three-quarters of patients with schizophrenia. This means that more people can live and function well in the community instead of needing care in mental hospitals.

Jodi's doctor prescribed one of these drugs for her. Finding the most effective one is mostly a matter of trial and error, but fortunately Jodi began to improve very quickly, and she did not experience any bothersome side effects except for a dry mouth. Her thinking seemed clearer, and she was able to concentrate on reading a book or watching a television program without becoming confused. The strange ideas she had expressed disappeared, and she wondered how she could have believed such a silly notion about her superhuman protective powers. By the end of the summer, she was able to go back to school. Taking medicine does not guarantee that the person will never have a relapse, but it decreases the chances.

Jodi's parents wanted to know about other kinds of treatment. They knew that before antipsychotic medicines were available, some risky and very unpleasant treatments were used. A friend of theirs believed that a special diet and vitamin therapy had helped him, but these are not proven treatments for schizophrenia.

Although *psychotherapy* (treatment by a mental health professional—a psychiatrist, psychologist, or other trained person) can help people with emotional problems, some kinds of psychotherapy can actually harm individuals with schizophrenia. Most experts believe that any therapy that involves the dredging up of forgotten ideas and disturbing feelings from the past makes the patients worse because it increases their anxiety and confusion. What they need is supportive therapy, that is, help in reorganizing their thinking and managing their lives.

Jodi was lucky. She spent only a week in the hospital, where tests were done and a program of medicine was started. She began to improve quickly, and she was able to go home. She visited the psychiatrist once a week, to talk and to make sure that her medication was working properly. The psychiatrist also spent some time with Jodi's family, giving them helpful suggestions and guidance. In the past, the family was seen as part of the problem, but now the family is considered part of the solution for the person with schizophrenia.

7.

Living with Depression

Are you feeling blue today? Everyone feels unhappy and depressed some of the time. This is not the kind of depression that is a mental illness. Unlike just feeling down once in a while, clinical depression is a bad feeling that will not go away. It does not improve over a short period of time or change when circumstances change. It interferes with the way people think, feel, and behave. Depressed people brood, cannot concentrate, and cannot enjoy normal pleasures. They have a poor self-image, sleep poorly or too much, and feel sad and empty. The constant feeling of hopelessness is more painful than can be imagined by those who do not suffer from it.

Depression seems to be on the rise in many countries in the twentieth century. In the past, many experts believed that very young children could not suffer from depression, but today they realize that the mental illness known as depression can appear at any age. Even infants can suffer from a kind of depression when they are neglected.

Doctors often find it difficult to diagnose depres-

Talent is not usually hindered by a mental illness.

sion in young children because they show a wide variety of symptoms. They do not always appear to be sad. Sometimes, it can be hard to tell which kids are really depressed and which are just rebelling against their parents as a part of the normal process of growing away from them.

Consider the case of Ken, who was six years old when his father deserted the family. His personality seemed to change after that. He lost interest in school, and his grades went down. He began to fight with other boys in his class, and he was mean to his little sister. He was caught stealing from stores and from his mother's wallet. Ken seemed angry and rebellious, not sad, so at first no one recognized that he was really suffering from depression.

Merrill was fifteen when she began feeling down in the dumps for long periods of time, but her parents thought she was being a typical teen. She stopped practicing her violin, even though she had long been planning a career in music and she showed great talent. She began spending more and more time locked in her room. When she started giving away her favorite books and knickknacks to friends, her parents took her to a doctor for counseling. The visits did not seem to help, so after three sessions Merrill refused to return. She felt she would never be happy again. Two weeks later, she cut her wrists because she felt too useless and worthless to live. The wrist cutting led to a short stay in the hospital where she started a program of medicine for depression. During the next few months, her therapist monitored her medication, and helped her to make some friends instead of isolating herself, to follow an exercise program, and to join a support group. This enabled her to return to school and her musical career. She was glad that she had not bled to death.

Ryan began feeling depressed at an early age. When he was in fourth grade, he decided he was ugly. He hated the way his hair grew. He threw away the shorts his parents bought him to wear in the summer because his knees were knobby. He avoided groups of people because he felt everyone was looking at him. He was sure no one could like such an ugly person as he was.

Ryan tried to start a chess club at school after a teacher learned that he was a good chess player. A number of boys and girls signed up to join, but Ryan felt he would not play well enough to help with the club. He stayed away from school the week the club was supposed to begin, so the club never started. When Ryan was asked to write an article for the school paper, he said he was too tired. Ryan really felt tired, but his parents thought he was just lazy. It seemed to Ryan that he could not do anything right.

Ryan thought selling drugs would make him popular, but he soon learned that the other kids were interested in him only for his drugs. He spent much of his time smoking marijuana in the field behind his house, watching television, and reading. He told himself he didn't need friends. After a while, he forgot how to make friends.

Ryan was not happy. In fact, he was very unhappy. The high he felt from drugs lasted only a short time. Actually, each high was followed by a period of depression. His periods of depression became longer until they seemed to take over his life.

Ryan was a very bright person, but he did not do

well in school. By seventh grade, he was too tired to go to school, and his parents let him stay in bed much of the day because they thought he must be sick even though their doctor could not find anything wrong with him. Ryan really was sick. He did not have much energy. He did not sleep well or eat well. He felt worthless and helpless. Ryan was suffering from depression, a serious mental illness that affects more than eleven million people in the United states each year. Among teens, 5 out of 100 are thought to be overwhelmed by depression.

The suffering of depressed people and their families is so great that it cannot be measured. Depression is one of the most painful kinds of mental illness, and it is one of the most common and unrecognized of all the kinds of mental disorders. This is especially tragic since depression is a treatable disease.

Studies have shown that depressed people have a disorder involving the chemicals in the brain that help transmit messages from one nerve cell to another. Depression tends to run in families, and it seems to be more common in women than in men.

People who suffer from depression that plays a major part in their lives need help from professionals. About 80 percent of these people can be helped with medicine and therapy. Unfortunately, only about one in three gets treatment. Many depressed people suffer needlessly because they do not know the symptoms of serious depression, have trouble asking for help, blame themselves, or don't know that treatments are available. Sometimes doctors do not recognize the problem.

How do you know if you or someone in your family is depressed? One or more of the following symptoms for this kind of mental illness is present nearly every day, all day, for at least two weeks:

- Loss of interest in things that were once enjoyable.
- Feeling sad, blue, or down in the dumps.
- Acting irritable or angry rather than sad, or showing aggressive or rebellious behavior, especially children and teenagers.

At least three of the following are usually present:

- Feeling worthless or guilty.
- Feeling slowed down or restless and unable to sit still.
- Thoughts of death or suicide.
- Problems concentrating, thinking, remembering, or making decisions.
- Trouble sleeping, or sleeping too much.
- Feeling bored all the time.
- Loss of energy or feeling tired all the time.
- Loss of appetite or eating more than usual.

Other symptoms are frequently present, too. Common ones include headaches, other aches and pains, digestive problems, sexual problems, and feeling worried, anxious, hopeless, and helpless. In more severe cases, the person may even have delusional beliefs, often centered on feeling unworthy.

Signs of depression may be different in different cultures. Instead of sadness, a person may have physical symptoms and complain of headaches, nerves, "imbalance," or of being "heartbroken." Often, depression is not recognized when it masquerades as physical problems such as tiredness, loss of appetite, and weight loss. The person may be subjected to numerous tests or referred for treatment that does not help the underlying depression. Sometimes, medical conditions—for example, stroke, hormone imbalance, infections, and some cancers—can mimic depression. Certain prescription medicines and some illegal drugs can also cause symptoms of depression. Depressed people occasionally try to medicate themselves by using alcohol or drugs like cocaine or amphetamine ("speed," "uppers"). This may give them temporary relief, but in the long run it is a dangerous practice.

Seasonal affective disorder is the name given to a type of depression that begins when the days start to get shorter and improves in the spring as the days become longer. Sitting under bright lights for several hours a day is the recommended treatment. Some fortunate individuals with this disorder are able to avoid it by spending the winter in Florida or in other sunny places.

Certain individuals have a form of depression that is milder than the more serious kind described earlier. It is called *dysthymic disorder.* It often begins in childhood and lasts for many years. The depression is so constant that it seems to be a part of the individual's personality. This disorder often overlaps with other kinds of emotional problems, such as anxiety disorder and disorders related to certain personality patterns. About 80 percent of people with dysthymia go on to develop more severe depression.

There are several factors that may contribute to depression: heredity, stressful events, personality, and deprivation or abuse early in life. No one really knows to what extent any of these plays a part. Some people seem more able than others to bounce back after negative life experiences; others are less resilient. The triggers for depression are more obvious in some cases than others.

If someone in your family is depressed, the most important thing you can do is encourage him or her to get treatment from a professional who can provide appropriate medicine and supportive therapy. Family and friends can provide much-needed support, love, and encouragement for those suffering the pain of depression. Treatment for depression is especially important because it can prevent the suicide of a person who feels so hopeless that he or she believes death is the only solution.

If you know someone who is at risk for suicide, you can tell the person that you understand how he or she feels, that as long as the person is alive, things can change, that you will help and stick by the person. But professional help is needed, too. You can suggest that the person call a suicide hotline (see your local phone book) and call yourself if the person refuses. You can ask for help from a school counselor, a doctor, or a teacher. Secrets about plans to commit suicide are secrets that should *not* be kept. One of the many myths about suicide is that talking about it makes it happen. Just the opposite seems to be true.

Some people with depression suffer from mood cycles. They feel very low for a while, and they feel unusually high at some other times. The high moods may last for several weeks or months, and there may be periods of normal mood between them. This kind of illness is called *bipolar disorder*. It is also called *manic-depressive disorder*.

Do you know someone who has any of the following symptoms?

- Feeling extremely elated or excited all the time. (This state is called euphoria.)
- Happy moods that switch quickly to irritable or angry moods.
- Needing little sleep.
- Having lots of ideas going through his or her head very quickly at one time.
- Having unrealistic ideas of greatly inflated self-importance.
- Feeling overly confident and capable of doing anything, despite lack of talent or experience.
- Feeling he or she has to keep moving.
- Appearing to have endless energy.
- Nonstop talking, joking, jumping from one idea to the next.
- Getting involved in behavior that is pleasurable but may be very risky, like wild buying sprees or sexual activities.

Having four of the above symptoms for at least one week may be a sign of a manic episode. Like depression without manic episodes, bipolar disorder tends to run in families and is caused by chemical imbalances in the brain. People who are manic-depressive need professional help, but their mood is so high they generally do not realize they need help. There are effective treatments for this kind of disorder. Seeking professional help promptly reduces the pain of the ill person and his or her family.

8.

Myths About Mental Illness

Myth 1: People with Mental Problems
Can Straighten Themselves Out
If They Really Want To

Nobody likes having problems or feeling unhappy and confused. If you broke a leg, no one would expect you to ignore the pain or know how to fix it yourself; you would go to a doctor. But many people think that if you are depressed and your life seems hopeless and bleak, you should somehow be able to talk yourself out of feeling this way. They might say, "You ought to feel lucky to have caring parents who give you a lot of love. They took you to Colorado for a wonderful week of skiing this year, and you don't even appreciate how good your life is." This kind of response often makes the person feel even worse. The fact is that people with depression cannot change the way they feel by using willpower. They are hurting and need help just as much as the person with the broken leg. There are special medicines for treating depression and other mental disorders, and there are psychiatrists, psychologists, and psychiatric social workers who can offer emotional support and therapy.

Myth 2: People with Mental Illness Are Usually Faking Their Symptoms to Gain Sympathy

This is rarely true, although people with mental illness sometimes use their problems as an excuse to depend on others too much or to avoid working, going to school, or socializing. This is called *secondary gain*. Often, people with physical illness such as asthma use their condition in the same way, as an excuse for not doing something. This does not necessarily mean that any of these people are faking their symptoms.

Myth 3: Mental Illness Is a Sign of Weakness

Mental illness is a disease, not a weakness.

Myth 4: All Mentally Ill People Are Apt to Be Violent

Most people with serious mental illness are more likely to be fearful and passive, rather than aggressive toward others. Unfortunately, when an extremely disturbed person commits a violent act, it is highly publicized in the newspapers and on television. The reality is that only a very small number of all the murders committed in the United States are committed by mentally ill people. The persistence of this myth causes many people to feel unnecessarily fearful or uncomfortable when they meet a person who has had a mental illness. The fact is that someone with no previous criminal record who has been treated for a mental illness is less likely to be arrested than the average citizen.

Myth 5: All Mental Illness Strikes Without Warning, So You Never Know Who Is Going to Become Crazy and Possibly Violent

There are almost always signs of serious mental illness that are signals for taking action and getting the person involved in treatment before the situation becomes serious. But family and friends often overlook early signs of illness. Sometimes the danger signs are not very obvious or they are considered normal behavior. Sometimes the mentally ill person does not share his or her thoughts and feelings with others, so no one else may be aware of any odd or bizarre ideas that person may have. A typical newspaper account of violent behavior by a mentally ill person includes observations by neighbors that the person was always very quiet, kept to himself or herself, and never bothered anyone. But closer scrutiny almost always reveals a troubled individual who may have been hearing voices telling him or her to do certain things, or who was holding a hidden anger inside that built up until it finally exploded. Knowing the danger signs could probably prevent many of these tragedies from occurring.

Myth 6: Mental Illness Is Caused by Poor Parenting

In the past, many psychiatrists thought that mothers, fathers, and disturbed family relationships could bring about mental illness. In the 1960s, a British psychoanalyst, Dr. R. D. Laing, suggested that schizophrenia is a healthy reaction to an insane world. According to this theory, the person diagnosed as mentally ill may actually be the sanest one in the family but is singled out as the scapegoat for the family's conflict. Such theories had no evidence to support them and have been discarded by all but a handful of mental health professionals. A sad consequence of these beliefs was that many parents suffered unnecessary guilt because they thought they had caused mental illness in their children. Scientific research has shown that serious mental illnesses may be the result of inherited tendencies, abnormalities in development of the brain, and disturbances in brain chemistry, but not bad parenting.

Myth 7: There Is No Such Thing as Mental Illness

Another analyst, Dr. Thomas Szasz, became known for his theory that schizophrenia and other serious mental disorders do not exist at all. He thought that schizophrenia is a fake disease, but experts now agree that mental disorders are real. Researchers have shown solid evidence that disorders such as schizophrenia and depression are caused by abnormalities in the brain.

Myth 8: Schizophrenia Means Split Personality, Like Different Minds in the Same Body

Schizophrenia has nothing to do with the condition known as multiple personality disorder. The term means splitting or fragmenting of the thought process. An individual with schizophrenia has a mind that works in fragments, one that is unable to make logical or appropriate connections.

Myth 9: Nervous Breakdown Is an Accepted Term for Mental Illness

Nervous breakdown or *case of nerves* are vague terms used by many people to describe an episode of emotional disturbance. But they are not medical terms or a diagnosis, and they are inaccurate because they may mean any one of a variety of mental conditions ranging from very serious to relatively minor.

Myth 10: Only People Who Are Crazy Go to a Psychiatrist

There are many kinds of mental disorders, some more serious than others. Qualified and specially trained mental health professionals can help people who are suffering from any kind of emotional disturbance. Depending on the problem, treatment may include medication. If someone is very seriously ill, he or she might be hospitalized or referred to a special residential treatment center. People often hesitate to seek help for mental problems because they are ashamed or afraid that others might think they are crazy. But there is nothing wrong with asking for help.

Myth 11: Psychiatrists Are Mind Readers

Psychiatrists have no extraordinary powers; they are people, just like everyone else, with varying degrees of expertise. But they have had special training in medical school and residency (several years of postgraduate education), and have learned how to diagnose and treat physical and mental disorders. They do not read your mind; they ask questions to learn about your thoughts and feelings.

Myth 12: Medicines for Treating Mental Illness Are Dangerous to Your Health

These medicines are no more dangerous than any others; all medicines pose a risk if used improperly. The medicines used to treat schizophrenia are sometimes called tranquilizers, but this is misleading, because their main action is to reduce the symptoms of the illness. Although some of the medicines cause drowsiness, not all of them produce this side effect.

Myth 13: People Who Have Had a Mental Illness Never Recover

All mental illnesses can be treated, and most people can be helped. Some may need long-term treatment, but others recover completely. When proper care and treatment are provided, almost everyone can expect to improve, and most can return to a normal life in the community.

Myth 14: People Who Have Been Treated for Mental Illness Cannot Hold a High-Level Job

There have been many famous people who had serious mental illness and yet excelled in fields such as politics, the arts, teaching, and science. Many have exceptional insight into the needs of the mentally ill. You might be surprised to discover that your favorite teacher was once treated for severe depression, or that the auto mechanic who always knows exactly where to find the trouble in your parents' car was hospitalized for two weeks with a diagnosis of schizophrenia as a teenager. Mental illness did not stop them from working or leading normal lives.

Myth 15: Young Children Do Not Suffer from Schizophrenia

Schizophrenia is not seen very often in children under the age of twelve, but it does occur. About 70 percent of the cases are boys.

Childhood schizophrenia is one of the most serious mental illnesses, and many children do not improve very much even with medicine and psychological treatment. Many children find it difficult to express their problems with words, so therapists ask them to draw pictures or give them dolls. The stories that children tell about their picture or dolls give the therapist clues about what troubles them. Play therapy is also used in treating children who have other disorders.

Fortunately, childhood schizophrenia is a rare illness, more rare than autism, and one-fiftieth as common as schizophrenia that starts in adulthood.

9.

How Can You Help?

*E*veryone suffers when someone in the family is mentally ill. Parents may blame each other, and brothers and sisters of the ill family member may blame themselves for causing the illness.

When someone in your family is mentally ill, you may suffer from *survivor guilt*. This kind of guilt is common when large numbers of people are killed in a disaster such as an earthquake. The question "Why didn't it happen to me?" plagues the survivors. Sometimes children deny themselves pleasures because a family member is sick. Feeling guilty because you are having a good time does not help the mentally ill person. Recognizing what you can do to help is far more important than feeling guilty.

Feeling grief over a loss is another common reaction to mental illness in the family. If you have a sick brother or sister, you may no longer count on him or her to be part of family celebrations, or to be ready to have fun with you, as in the past. In the case of a sick parent, he or she may not be able to take care of you or be understanding when you have problems.

Many children feel neglected and jealous because their parents give too much attention to a brother or sister who is mentally ill. This is a difficult problem for kids and parents. Some kids hide their feelings about these problems. They bury them until some small incident triggers a big explosion of anger. This rage is often misunderstood by other family members, and it makes things worse. Talking about feelings before an explosion builds up is a better way of dealing with the problem, and it makes life better for the whole family.

Occasionally kids who misbehave or get into trouble are really feeling angry or depressed underneath but cannot express their feelings by talking. Jed was a good student and never had any problems until his sister became depressed and tried to commit suicide. He felt pained by his sister's illness, and he was angry because his parents were so concerned about his sister that they were ignoring him. Jed began neglecting his schoolwork and hanging out with kids who were dealing drugs. Smoking marijuana made him feel better and dealing drugs made him feel more important for a short time, but then his teachers and parents found out what was happening. They were upset and

A Few Facts
Severe Mental Illnesses Are:

• *Biological brain diseases* that interfere with normal brain chemistry. Genetic factors may create a predisposition in some people, and life stresses may trigger the onset of symptoms.

• *Very common.* In one year, 30.7 million Americans are affected. That's 16.7 percent of the population. Over 3 million children and adolescents suffer from these illnesses.

• *Equal opportunity diseases*, striking families from all walks of life, regardless of age, race, income, religion, or education.

• *Devastating to ill persons and their families.* One's thinking, feeling, and relating are disrupted, seriously reducing the ability to live a normal life. All family members are affected.

• *Treatable!* Appropriate medical care and rehabilitation enable many people to recover enough to live productive lives.

Are Not:

• *Anybody's fault.* They are not caused by poor parenting or weak character.

• *Preventable or curable at this time.* Great advances have been made in understanding brain functioning, but not enough is known yet to prevent or cure serious mental illnesses.

• *Hopeless!* These illnesses present difficult challenges, but help is available. Support, education, and a community of friends who understand can make family life satisfying and meaningful again.

Source: National Alliance for the Mentally Ill.

disappointed, and Jed realized that this was not the kind of attention he wanted.

When a family member is mentally ill, children often worry that they might become ill as well. They and their parents look at every quirk or bad mood as possible signs of sickness, even though they probably are the usual temporary and insignificant upsets that happen to everyone.

People with schizophrenia often blame their parents. Nora is convinced that her illness began because her father spent too much time at work and was always too tired to pay attention to her. She complains that her mother and father both favored her younger sister. Nora's parents were once told by a psychiatrist that they did not communicate well with their children. Now they worry and feel guilty about being bad parents.

Getting rid of blame and guilt is a big step toward developing the right attitude about mental illness. Just knowing that they cannot cure a family member who is ill helps others in the family. The sick individual needs the help of a psychiatrist and other people trained in the field of mental illness. It is important to recognize that you cannot change that person's behavior, but you can be helpful and supportive. It does no good to tell the ill person to act normal. Being unrealistic about what an ill individual is able to do (for instance, pressuring someone to return to college) creates stress and is not helpful.

Getting upset about problems makes things worse for the mentally ill family member. Studies have shown that mentally ill people living with their families do better when the family does not become too emotional. You can talk about problems in an open, straightforward way but at the same time keep a kind and tolerant attitude.

Shame is another feeling that is common when someone in the family is mentally ill. Terry's grandmother always made Cousin Hattie go to her room when anyone came to the house, so visitors never had the opportunity to hear about her imagined secret life as an undercover agent for the FBI.

Everybody in one small town thought that Mr. and Mrs. Green had no children. But one day, a handsome young man named Robert Green was admitted to the state hospital. Robert was quiet and polite, but he seemed awkward and uneasy with other people. He didn't talk much, and he had some odd ideas. He said that he lived alone in a furnished room and spent his time watching television. He had no friends and rarely went out. His parents paid his rent and sent him money for food, but they never visited him and would not allow him in their house. They had an unlisted telephone number that Robert did not know. He had little contact with them, except on the few occasions when he became upset and tried to visit them, banging on the door and shouting, disturbing the neighbors. The Greens called the police, who made Robert leave and go back to his furnished room.

Robert's parents told the hospital social worker

that after Robert had a "nervous breakdown" in high school, they allowed him to drop out, even though he had previously been a good student. They never consulted a doctor or mental health professional because they were too embarrassed. So the Greens hid him away, and he became a hermit, living alone with his strange ideas, without anything else to occupy his mind.

Robert could have been helped with medication and psychological support. He probably would have been able to finish school, hold a job, and keep his good relationship with his parents. But the Greens were so ashamed that Robert had a mental illness that they were willing to pretend their only child did not exist.

Although troubled relatives are not usually hidden from society the way they were in the past, many kids would like to hide them when their friends visit. But true friends are often more accepting of the situation than you might expect. Those who are not accepting are not worth having as friends.

In his book *Surviving Schizophrenia*, psychiatrist E. Fuller Torrey notes that a sense of humor is very helpful in achieving the right attitude about mental illness. Having a sense of humor does not mean laughing at the ill person; it means laughing with him or her. Dr. Torrey tells of one family with a schizophrenic son who had a relapse of illness requiring hospitalization every fall. The standing family joke with the son was that he always carved his Halloween pumpkins in the hospital.

Joining a support group is a great help for families of the mentally ill. The National Alliance for the Mentally Ill (NAMI) has a helpline you can call for information about the support group closest to you. The number is 1-800-950-NAMI. Among their services is special support for brothers and sisters of mentally ill people, called Sibling Network.

Increased understanding that mentally ill people should not be blamed for their conditions any more than diabetics should be blamed for having diabetes has made their diseases more acceptable. There is still a long way to go to remove the stigma that prevents large numbers from seeking help. Learning more about mental illness and getting support from others can help everyone deal with a problem that touches millions of families.

Glossary

affect: term that refers to a feeling state or emotion such as sadness or anger. Affect may be flat (little or no sign of any emotion) or inappropriate (no relationship between the emotion a person is feeling and what he or she is saying or thinking). Affect is to weather as mood is to climate; it refers to shifts in emotional weather. In contrast, mood is a long-lasting state. (See mood.)

agoraphobia: anxiety about being in places or situations alone, usually crowded places or traveling in a bus or train; the anxiety stems from fear of having a panic attack away from home.

Alzheimer's disease: type of dementia that is progressive. Most prevalent in people over sixty-five.

ambivalence: indecision about how one feels; inability to choose between conflicting feelings.

anorexia: an eating disorder, occurring most often in young women who have a distorted body image (thinking they are too fat when they are actually thin) and diet excessively, refusing to maintain a healthy body weight. Low weight is maintained through starvation and excessive exercise. It can result in loss of bone, heart and kidney damage, disturbances in body chemistry, anemia, and even death.

antipsychotic drugs: specific medicines that do not cure but alleviate the symptoms of mental illness such as the delusions and hallucinations of schizophrenia.

anxiety: feelings of uneasiness and tension, due to fear of some danger about to happen. Sometimes the person does not know why he or she is afraid.

attention-deficit/hyperactivity disorder (AD/HD): pattern of symptoms that include inattention, increased activity, inability to finish tasks, impulsivity, distractibility, and restlessness. This disorder begins before age seven and causes problems in the family and at school. Sometimes difficult to distinguish between AD/HD and normal, active young child.

autism: rare brain disorder evident before the age of three, sometimes recognized in infancy. Symptoms include emotional detachment, inability to relate to others, severe abnormalities of speech and communication, and more interest in objects than in people.

bipolar disorder: also called manic-depressive disorder. Mood disorder in which there are episodes of serious depression, or "lows," and episodes of mania, or "highs."

bulimia: eating disorder marked by extreme concern about body weight and shape and by episodes of binge eating (eating huge amounts of food) followed by inducing vomiting or taking laxatives to avoid weight gain. It can result in loss of tooth enamel, damage to stomach and esophagus, and sometimes death. Weight is usually normal.

catatonia: withdrawn, unresponsive state, often with refusal to move, or strange movements or postures.

chronic: continuing over an extended period of time (usually years). A person with a chronic illness may have long periods without major symptoms, but the symptoms recur occasionally.

commitment: involuntary hospitalization. This is a legal procedure requiring proof that because of a mental illness, the person is a danger to him-/herself or others or cannot care for him-/herself.

compulsion: the urge to perform a certain behavior.

conduct disorder: persistent pattern of behavior in children or adolescents, in which there are serious violations of rules, disregard of the rights of others, such as bullying or cruelty to others, destruction of property belonging to others, stealing, running away from home, and truancy.

delusion: bizarre or false belief not ordinarily accepted by other members of the person's culture or religion; for example, "I am king of the universe," "aliens from another planet are controlling my mind." A person with delusional ideas cannot be convinced that these beliefs are incorrect.

dementia: condition marked by memory loss, difficulty in learning new information, and loss of intellectural skills and mental abilities that the individual had previously.

depression: see mood disorders.

dysthymic disorder: form of depression that begins early in life, is chronic, and seems to be part of the individual's personality.

eating disorder: severe disturbance in eating behavior, either anorexia or bulimia or a combination of both. Bingeing is another, less serious form of eating disorder that does not involve fasting, vomiting, purging, or excessive exercise. It involves occasional episodes of excessive overeating.

echolalia: irrational repetition of word or sentence spoken by another person.

echopraxia: senseless, automatic imitation of movements or gestures made by another person.

electroencephalogram (EEG): tracing of electrical impulses originating in the brain. Electrodes are attached to various parts of the head and connected to a recording device.

euphoria: elated or high mood state.

genetic: having to do with genes, which are blueprints for traits passed from parents to children through the sperm and the egg cells. Some traits of this kind include eye color, blood type, and the risk for developing certain illnesses, including schizophrenia and depression.

hallucination: false experience of the senses (feeling, smell, taste, vision, or sound). Many people with schizophrenia hear voices or sounds.

insanity: term sometimes used to mean mental illness. It is actually a legal term (not a medical term) used by judges and lawyers. The definition sets out standards for determining whether a person has a mental illness that impairs his/her ability to know right from wrong.

magnetic resonance imaging (MRI): method of visualizing internal structures in the head or body by placing the person in a strong magnetic field and recording the energy given off by atomic particles in the body parts being studied. More accurate than X rays and has no known risk.

mania: see mood disorders.

manic-depressive disorder: see bipolar disorder and mood disorders.

medications: drugs (medicines) prescribed by a physician or nurse practitioner; sometimes called meds.

mood: emotional state that influences a person's view of the world.

mood disorders: serious disturbances of mood, which include depression (very low) and mania (very high). In some cases, a person fluctuates between depression (persistent sadness, lack of appetite, loss of enthusiasm, fatigue, feelings of worthlessness) and mania (euphoria, rapid speech, feelings of great power or attractiveness, agitation, decreased need for sleep, irresponsible behavior). This is called bipolar disorder or manic-depressive disorder.

neuroleptic drugs: see psychotropic drugs.

obsession: persistent idea, thought, image, or impulse that is not logical, often resulting in compulsive behavior.

obsessive-compulsive disorder (OCD): disorder that usually includes compulsive behavior as well as uncontrollable obsessive thoughts.

panic disorder: disorder marked by sudden attacks of intense fear or discomfort, with symptoms such as pounding heart, sweating, feelings of choking, shortness of breath, or dizziness, and fear of losing control or going crazy.

paranoia: extreme mistrust and suspiciousness that causes a person to believe that other people or forces are observing him or her, influencing events, or planning some kind of harm.

phobia: excessive, unreasonable fear of specific objects or situations. Some common phobias include fear of heights, fear of flying, and fear of snakes.

psychiatrist: medical doctor who has received specialty training in the diagnosis and treatment of mental illness. Psychiatrists can provide medicine and conduct psychotherapy.

psychoanalysis: a type of intensive psychotherapy that originated with Sigmund Freud, based on the theory that some mental illness is caused by childhood experiences. The treatment may take years, involving three to five sessions a week with an analyst who has special training in this type of therapy. It involves the recall of memories and feelings that have been buried in the unconscious part of the mind.

psychologist: person with a graduate degree in psychology, qualified to do psychological testing and psychotherapy.

psychosis: mental state in which there is a serious defect in the ability to recognize what is real. For example, delusions, hallucinations, or disjointed thinking are evidence of psychosis.

Certain experiences may be considered normal in one culture and psychotic in another.

psychotherapy: treatment of emotional problems or mental disorder through talking with a mental health professional. The aims vary according to the needs of the individual but often include such goals as enabling the patient to better understand him-/herself, to improve communication and relationships with others, to increase self-esteem, to change self-defeating behavior, and to offer support during difficult times.

psychotic: adjective used to describe speech and behavior, or a person with psychosis.

retrovirus: virus that inserts its genes into the genetic material of the host cell. The virus may remain hidden and inactive for a long time, but may give rise to disease years after infection.

seasonal affective disorder: type of depression that occurs during the winter season, when the daylight hours are shorter. The use of bright lights alleviates the symptoms.

schizophrenia: group of related disorders that affect the ability to think clearly, resulting in confusion and inappropriate behavior. Delusions and hallucinations are common. Schizophrenia is a disorder of thinking rather than of mood.

secondary gain: advantages gained by a person who has an illness or disability, that may be an incentive for avoiding activities or remaining dependent on others. For example, a person with agoraphobia whose mother drives her everywhere she needs to go may be reluctant to get treatment because she would no longer have an excuse for relying on her mother to care for her.

siblings: brothers and sisters.

social worker: person with special training in social work, which includes case management (coordinating treatment, helping to obtain financial benefits and medical or legal assistance, helping to find a place to live) and often counseling.

therapy: treatment of disease or incapacity.

tic: rapid, uncontrollable, repetitive movement or sound.

Tourette's syndrome: rare disease defined by involuntary tics and verbalizations.

waxy flexibility: condition sometimes found in people with catatonia. The individual maintains an immobile posture, but his or her arms or legs can be moved to a different position, where they remain.

word salad: speech that is totally disorganized and incomprehensible, composed of strings of unrelated words or phrases.

For Further Information

American Anorexia/Bulimia Association, Inc.
418 East 76th Street, 6th floor
New York, NY 10021

Anorexia Nervosa and Related Eating Disorders, Inc.
P.O. Box 5102
Highland Park
Eugene, OR 97405

Anxiety Disorders Association of America
Department A
6000 Executive Boulevard
Rockville, MD 20852

Attention Deficit Disorder Network
475 Hillside Avenue
Needham, MA 02194

Autism Society of America
7910 Woodmont Avenue,
Suite 650
Bethesda, MD 20814

**Center for Mental Health
Services**
Office of Consumer, Family,
and Public Information
5600 Fishers Lane
Rockville, MD 20857

**Center for the Study of
Anorexia and Bulimia**
1 West 91st Street
New York, NY 10024

**Children and Adults with
Attention Deficit Disorder**
499 Northwest 70th Avenue,
Suite 308
Plantation, FL 33317

**National Alliance for the
Mentally Ill (NAMI)**
200 North Glebe Road,
Suite 1015
Arlington, VA 22203

**National Association of
Anorexia Nervosa and
Associated Disorders**
P.O. Box 7
Highland Park, IL 60035

**National Depressive and Manic
Depressive Association**
730 North Franklin, Suite 501
Chicago, IL 60610

**National Eating Disorder
Organization**
445 East Granville Road
Worthington, OH 43085

**National Foundation for
Depressive Illness**
P.O. Box 2257
New York, NY 10116

**National Institute of Mental
Health**
Information Resources and
Inquiries Branch
5600 Fishers Lane
Rockville, MD 20857

**National Mental Health
Association**
1021 Prince Street
Alexandria, VA 22314

**National Institute of
Neurological Disorders and
Stroke**
9000 Rockville Pike, Bldg. 31
Bethesda, MD 20892

**OCD (Obsessive Compulsive
Disorder) Foundation, Inc.**
P.O. Box 70
Milford, CT 06460

Phobics Anonymous
P.O. Box 1180
Palm Springs, CA 92263

Tourette Syndrome
Association
42-40 Bell Boulevard
Bayside, NY 11361

For Further Reading

Dinner, Sherry. *Nothing to Be Ashamed Of: Growing Up with Mental Illness in Your Family.* New York: Lothrop, Lee and Shepard, 1982.

Gordon, M. *Jumpin' Johnny, Get Back to Work! A Child's Guide to ADHD/Hyperactivity.* DeWitt, N.Y.: GSI Publications, 1991.

Greenberg, Harvey Roy. *Emotional Illness in Your Family.* New York: Macmillan, 1989.

Hipp, Earl. *Feed Your Head.* Center City, Minn.: Hazelden, 1991.

Hyde, Margaret O. *The Homeless: Profiling the Problem.* Hillside, N.J.: Enslow, 1989.

Kubersky, Rachel. *Everything You Need to Know About Eating Disorders: Anorexia and Bulimia.* New York: Rosen Publishing Group, 1992.

Lundy, Allan. *Diagnosing and Treating Mental Illness.* New York: Chelsea House, 1990.

Moe, Barbara. *Coping with Eating Disorders.* New York: Rosen Publishing Group, 1991.

Quinn, Patricia, and Judith Stern. *Putting on the Brakes: Young People's Guide to Attention Deficit Disorder.* New York: Magination Press, 1991.

Riley, Jocelyn. *Crazy Quilt.* New York: William Morrow, 1984.

Silverstein, Herman. *Teenage Depression.* New York: Franklin Watts, 1990.

Simpson, Carolyn. *Coping with Emotional Disorders.* New York: Rosen Publishing Group, 1991.

Time-Life Books. *Mind and Brain: Journey Through Mind and Body.* Alexandria, Va.: Time-Life Books, 1993.

Index

129

131